Mozart the Clinic Cat

FIRST FANCY GROOM

by Delicia Miller

illustrated by Maxine Kuepfer

ISBN: 978-1-997584-00-1
Contact the publisher for Library and Archives Canada catalogue information.

aR

ALANNA RUSNAK PUBLISHING
a division of Chicken House Press
chickenhousepress.ca

It was another start to
a lively Monday morning.

As the clinic lights were turning on, the grooming department was already busy welcoming many excited guests.

Mozart watched from afar
as Pedro eagerly met the groomer.

"I wonder what is so exciting over there?"
Mozart thought to himself.

"It always seems way too noisy for a nap."

Just then, out of the corner of his eye, he noticed the dreaded brush. "Not the brush again!" Mozart groaned.

The Clinic staff tried to brush out Mozart's matted fur, but he was never impressed.

If they brushed him while he was sitting, he ran away. If they brushed him laying down, he would bite at the brush.

And even if they tried brushing him while cuddling him, he would kick them until they stopped.

When the receptionist scooped Mozart up, she didn't try to brush him. Instead, she carried him towards the hustling and bustling grooming department and handed him to the groomer.

As they entered the grooming room, Mozart was greeted by many dogs eagerly awaiting their grooms. "What's going on?" Mozart wondered. "I normally help manage the clinic."

"Hey Mozart!" yelled Pedro. "Maybe you're being groomed too."

"Groomed? What does it mean?" Mozart asked, quite concerned.

"When I get groomed, they start by giving me a warm bath," exclaimed Lupini.

As the groomer turned on the taps, Mozart imagined what having a bath would feel like.

Wet and soapy?
NOPE!

Mozart jumped out of her arms to run away.

The groomer
quickly turned
off the
running water,
scooped up
Mozart, and
reassured him
that they
would skip the
bath today.

"SHAVE! SHAVE! SHAVE!"
the dogs chanted.

"When I get groomed, she gives me a nice shave down my back and sides!" announced Sunny.

As the noisy clippers turned on, Mozart anxiously waited to see what would happen next.

"Huh," Mozart sighed. "This actually feels quite nice."

Mozart relaxed as the groomer shaved down his back and his sides.

"LEGS! LEGS! LEGS!"
the dogs chanted.

"When I get groomed, she shaves my legs and cuts the fur around my paws," explained Pedro.

Mozart watched as the clippers moved down his back legs, but they only shaved half way.

And then she moved the clippers towards his front legs.

"Okay, now this feels different and I don't know if I like it," Mozart said as the groomer shaved his armpits.

Mozart was pleasantly surprised when she stopped there and did not shave down his front legs or paws.

"FACE! FACE! FACE!"
the dogs chanted.

"When I get groomed, she shapes my beautiful head with scissors," Rogue proudly exclaimed.

Mozart waited for the scissors to be picked up but was surprised when he got scooped up instead. The groomer cuddled Mozart and praised him for being such a good boy for his groom as she walked him back over to the clinic.

The clinic staff gathered together in excitement to see Mozart's new hair cut.

As the groomer set him down on the table, Mozart began to stretch out and look around to see what he thought too.

"Wow, this looks different. It feels good, but did someone turn the heat down in here?" Mozart asked.

He walked towards the staff, looking for cuddles.

It was no surprise that the clinic staff had already thought of Mozart and had his bed ready for him.

Mozart kneaded the blankets, had one big

SSTTRREETTCCHH

and a very loud
YAWN
before curling up into a ball on his warm,
cozy bed.

"That was a busier morning than I had planned," Mozart
sighed. "I think I'll take a little nap."

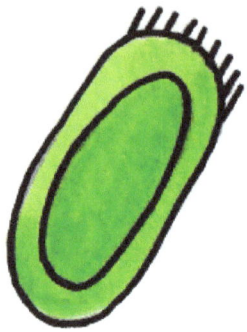

Devotional:

Mozart needed his fur to be taken care of, but he didn't enjoy being brushed. His fur tangled up so much they decided that a groom would be best for him. Mozart was worried, he didn't know what that meant, he didn't understand what was going to happen. The dogs in the grooming area knew Mozart was worried and instead of staying quiet or saying things to make him more scared, they encouraged Mozart by explaining things and showing how great having a groom is.

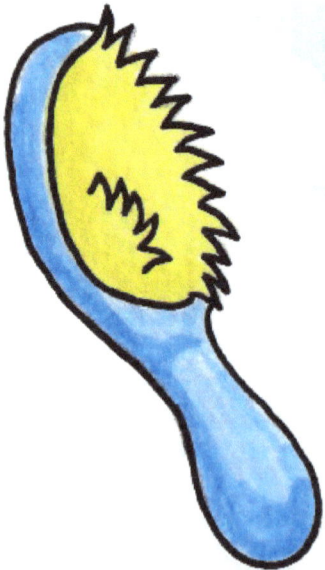

What does the word encourage mean?

When we encourage someone, we are giving support, hope or strengthening someone's confidence.

"Anxiety weighs down the heart, but a kind word cheers it up."

Proverbs 12:25

When we are worried about something, but someone shares a kind word or brings us encouragement, this can help us start to feel better. What if the dogs didn't say anything to Mozart but just watched him fearfully receive his first groom? What if the dogs decided to share scary grooming stories? Neither of these responses would have helped Mozart, they would have made him more fearful of the groom.

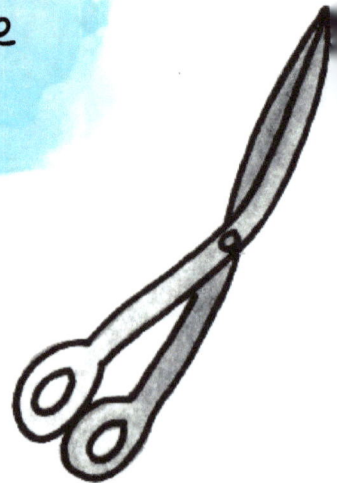

Our words matter, and the way we speak to others matter. Next time you know someone is worried, scared, or concerned about something let's use our words to bring hope, give support, and to strengthen their confidence.

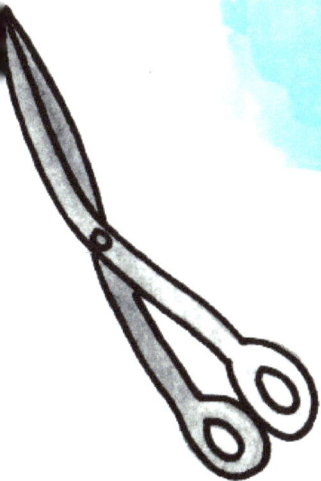

Rogue

Pedro

Lupini

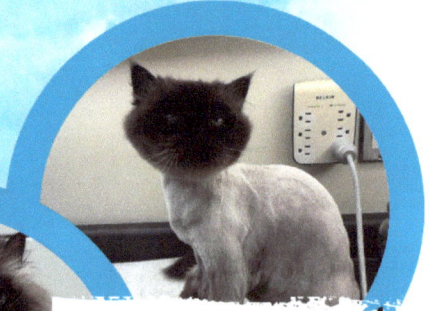

Sunny

Mozart

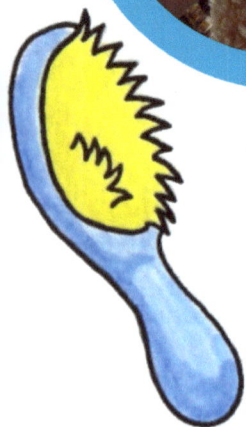

Mozart the Clinic Cat

Look for the other books in this series

NO PLACE TO SLEEP
THE LOST BUNNY
THE CHRISTMAS VET

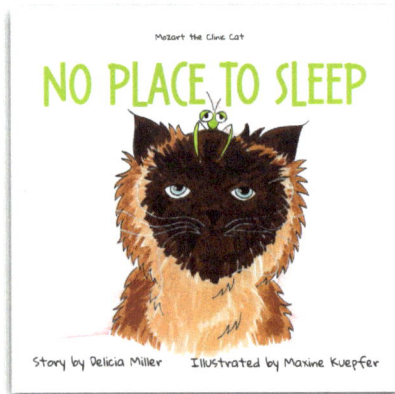

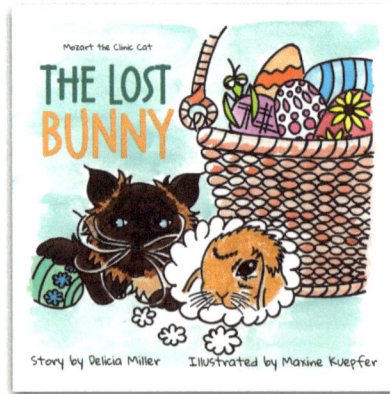

Mozart the Clinic Cat

NO PLACE TO SLEEP

Story by Delicia Miller   Illustrated by Maxine Kuepfer

Mozart the Clinic Cat

THE LOST BUNNY

Story by Delicia Miller   Illustrated by Maxine Kuepfer

THE CHRISTMAS VET

Story by Delicia Miller   Illustrated by Maxine Kuepfer

www.ingramcontent.com/pod-product-compliance
Lightning Source LLC
Chambersburg PA
CBHW042103040426

42448CB00002B/117